SCHOLASTIC

Let's Find Out

My REBUS Reader

I0890053

How Do Animals Beat the Heat?

by Mark Bailey

SCHOLASTIC INC.
New York Toronto London Auckland Sydney New Delhi Hong Kong

How do  beat the heat?

lions

They rest under a .

tree

How do  elephants beat the heat?

They spray  water.

How do  pigs beat the heat?

They roll in the  mud.

How do  beat the heat?

mountain goats

They shed their winter  .

coats

How do  prairie dogs beat the heat?

They go into a  hole.

How do  beat the heat?
desert owls

They hide in a  .
cactus

How do  kids beat the heat?

They drink  water, run through 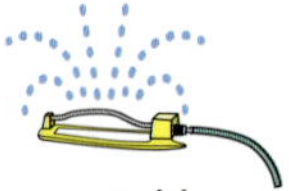 sprinklers, and eat  ice pops!